A Voyage to the Bottom of the Sea

Words by Norman C. Habel
Pictures by Jim Roberts

Concordia Publishing House

P A PURPLE PUZZLE TREE BOOK

COPYRIGHT © 1972
CONCORDIA PUBLISHING HOUSE,
ST. LOUIS, MISSOURI
CONCORDIA PUBLISHING HOUSE LTD.,
LONDON, E. C. 1
MANUFACTURED IN THE
UNITED STATES OF AMERICA
ALL RIGHTS RESERVED

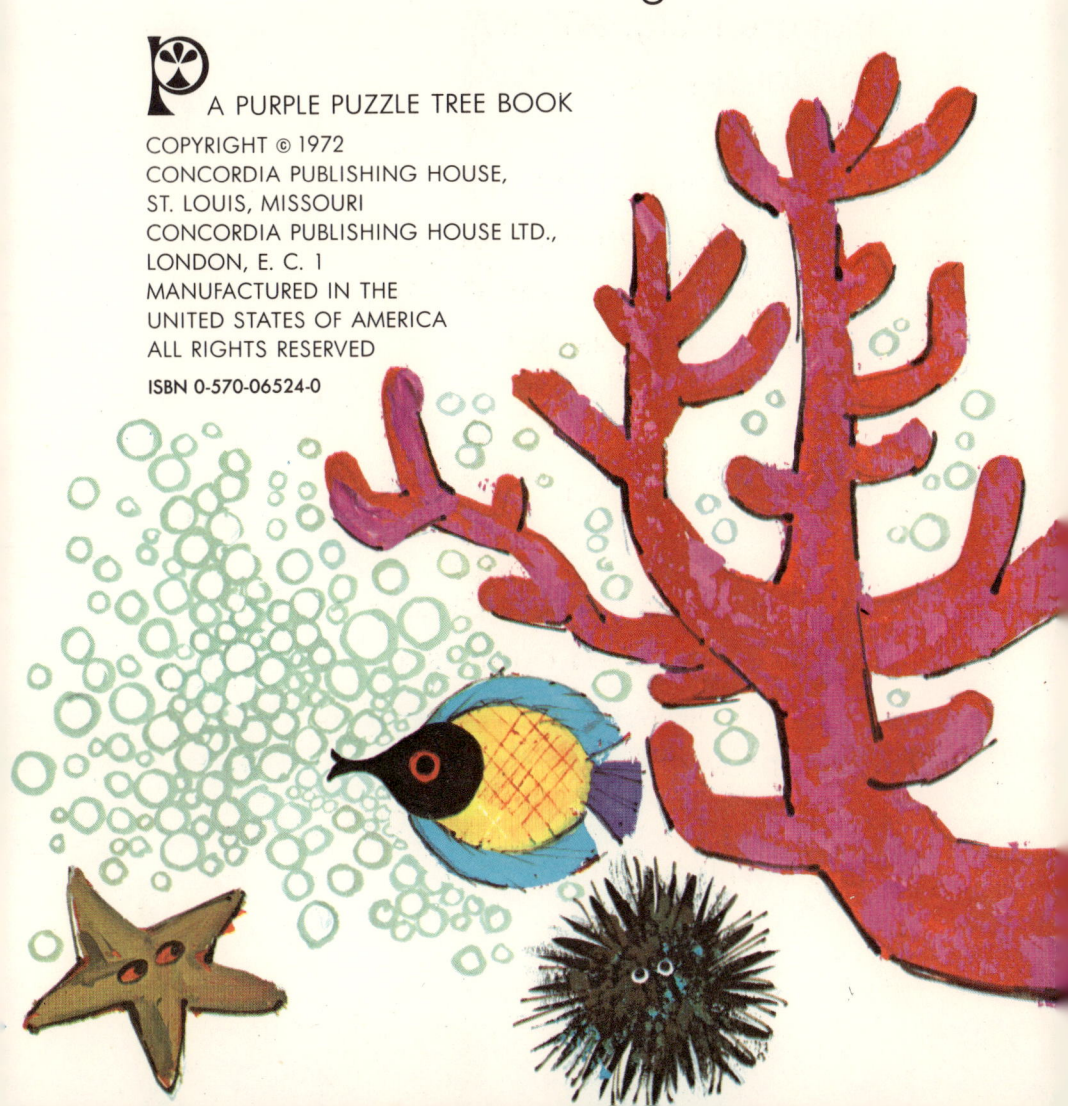

ISBN 0-570-06524-0

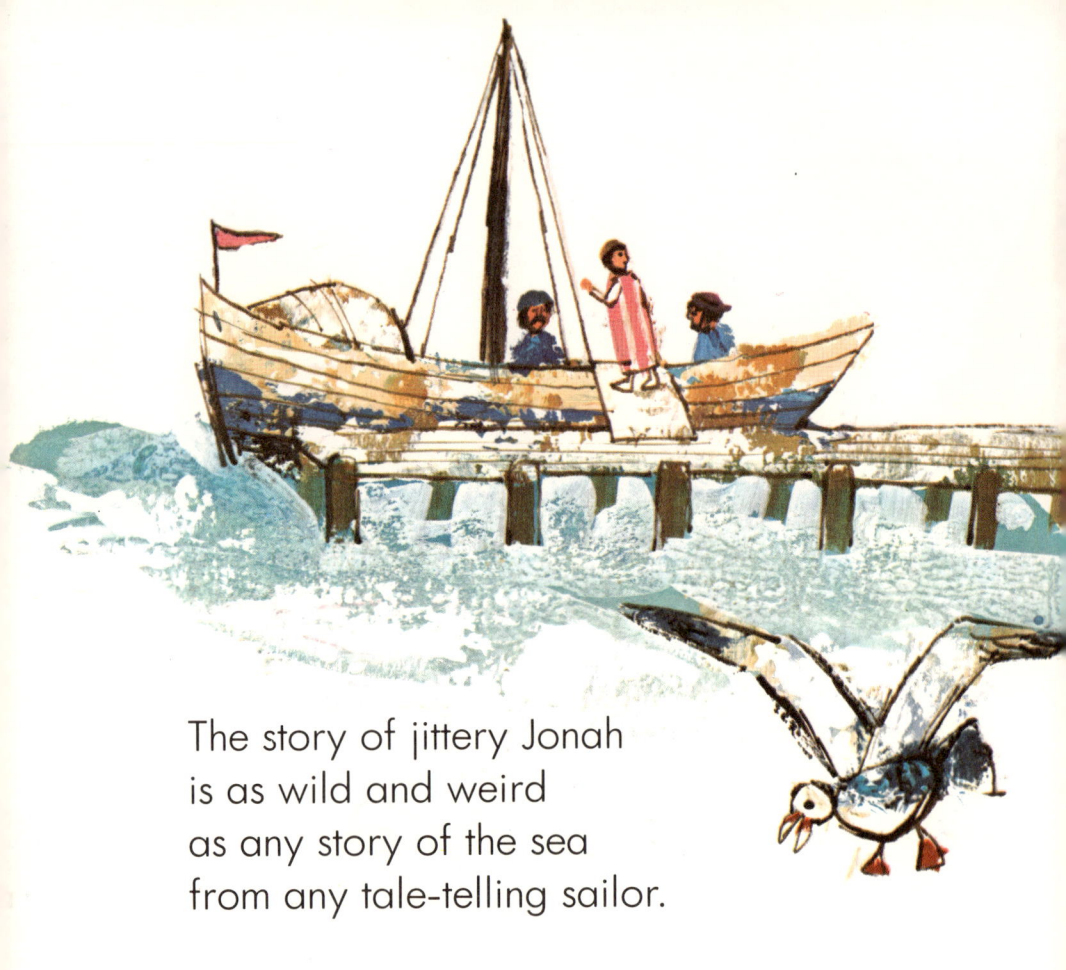

The story of jittery Jonah
is as wild and weird
as any story of the sea
from any tale-telling sailor.

Jonah was a prophet of God
who didn't like to preach.
But God had given orders
to "Go and preach in Nineveh,
that great big, evil city
far, far away."

Well, Jonah got the jitters
and ran to save his skin.
He took a ship to sail away,
far away from Israel,
and far away from God.

Or so he thought!

Then a weird thing happened
as the ship sailed out to sea.
A storm blew up from out of nowhere
and threw the ship around
as if it were a cardboard box
filled with helpless toys.

And still today sailors sing
of the storm and jittery Jonah:

   Winds blew down from out of nowhere,
   Storms raged in from out of nowhere,
   Waves roared up from out of nowhere
   After jittery Jonah.
   OOEEEE, winds were blowing,
   OOEEEE, storms were raging,
   OOEEEE, waves were roaring
   After jittery Jonah.

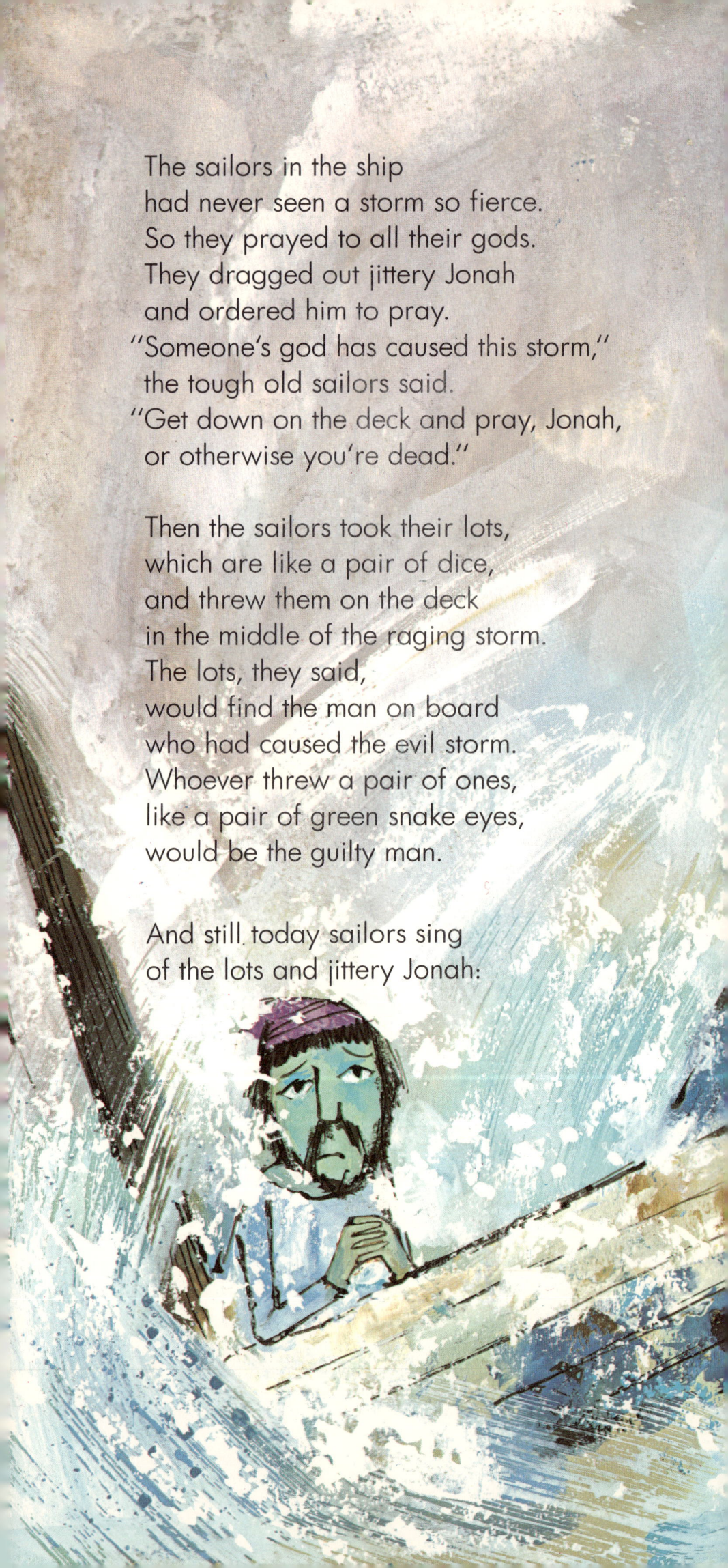

The sailors in the ship
had never seen a storm so fierce.
So they prayed to all their gods.
They dragged out jittery Jonah
and ordered him to pray.
"Someone's god has caused this storm,"
the tough old sailors said.
"Get down on the deck and pray, Jonah,
or otherwise you're dead."

Then the sailors took their lots,
which are like a pair of dice,
and threw them on the deck
in the middle of the raging storm.
The lots, they said,
would find the man on board
who had caused the evil storm.
Whoever threw a pair of ones,
like a pair of green snake eyes,
would be the guilty man.

And still today sailors sing
of the lots and jittery Jonah:

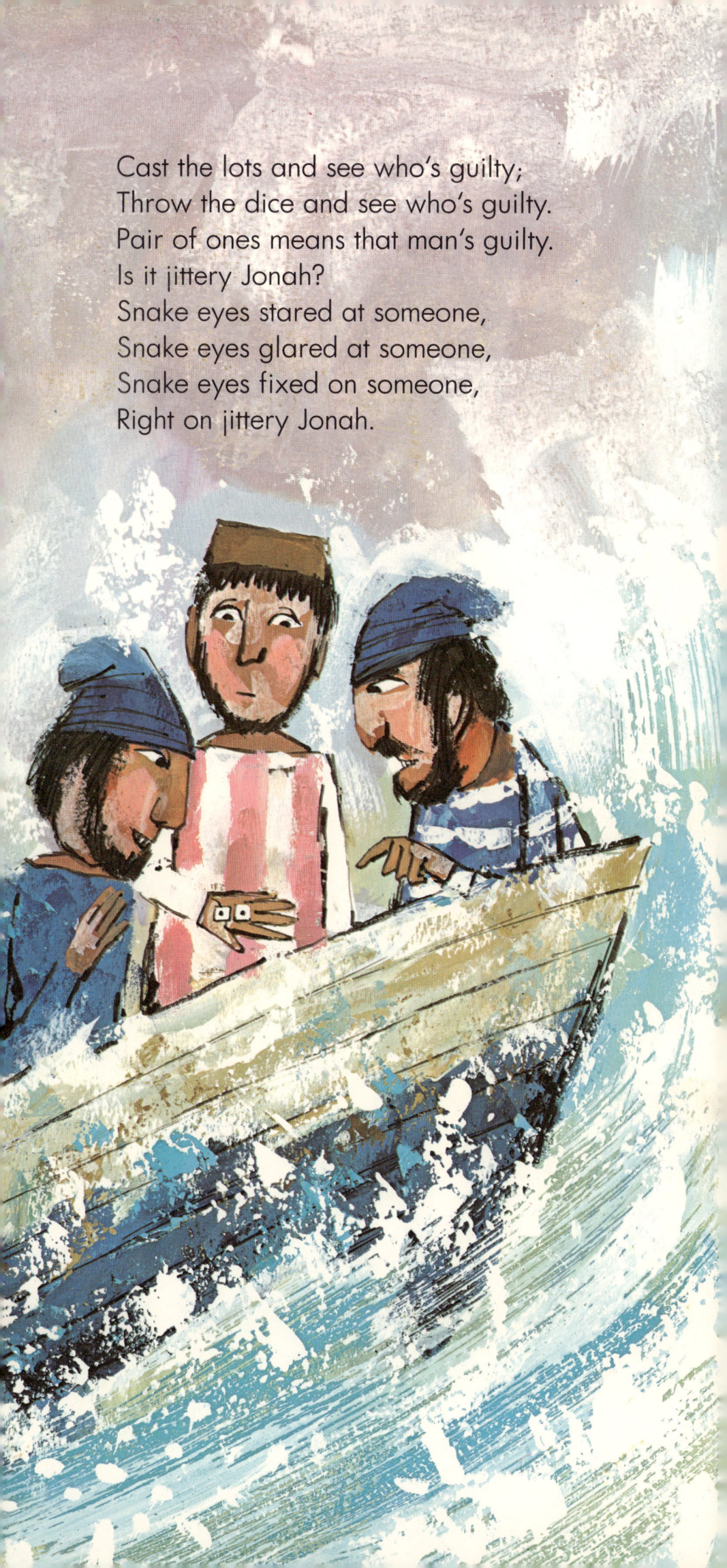

Cast the lots and see who's guilty;
Throw the dice and see who's guilty.
Pair of ones means that man's guilty.
Is it jittery Jonah?
Snake eyes stared at someone,
Snake eyes glared at someone,
Snake eyes fixed on someone,
Right on jittery Jonah.

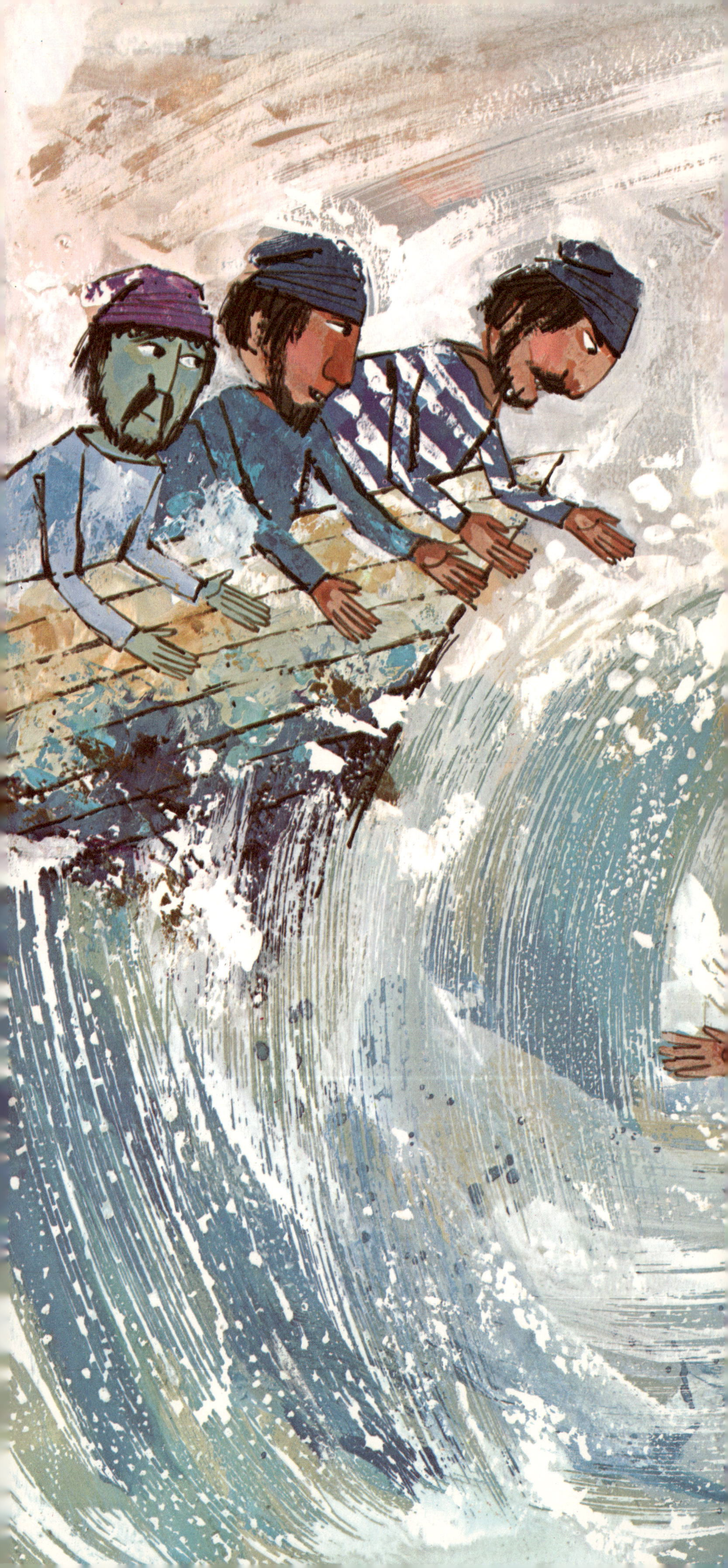

The lots said Jonah was to blame,
and Jonah really was.
"My God is chasing me," said Jonah,
"because I will not preach
to a great big, evil city
far, far away."

They threw poor jittery Jonah
into the raging sea.
And, just like that,
the sea was calm
and the waves were flat,
like a wide, green-blue carpet
or a shining green-blue mat.

Then a strange thing happened
as all the sailors watched.
A big and monstrous fish
came roaring from the deep.
And still today sailors sing
of the fish and jittery Jonah:

    Monstrous fish from out of nowhere,
    Like a whale from out of nowhere,
    Roaring up from out of nowhere
    After jittery Jonah.
    Oops there, in goes Jonah.
    Oops there, down goes Jonah.
    Oops there, where is Jonah?
    Poor old jittery Jonah.

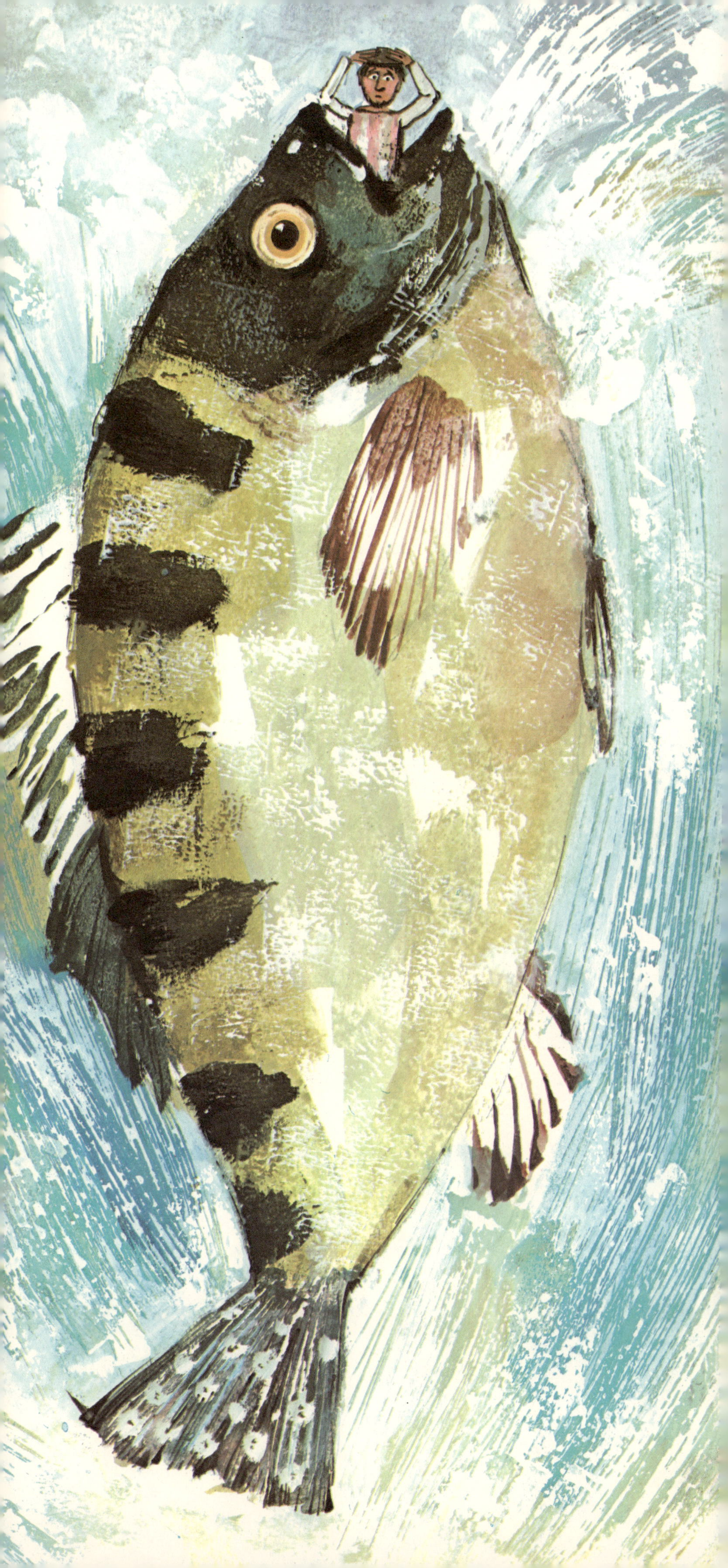

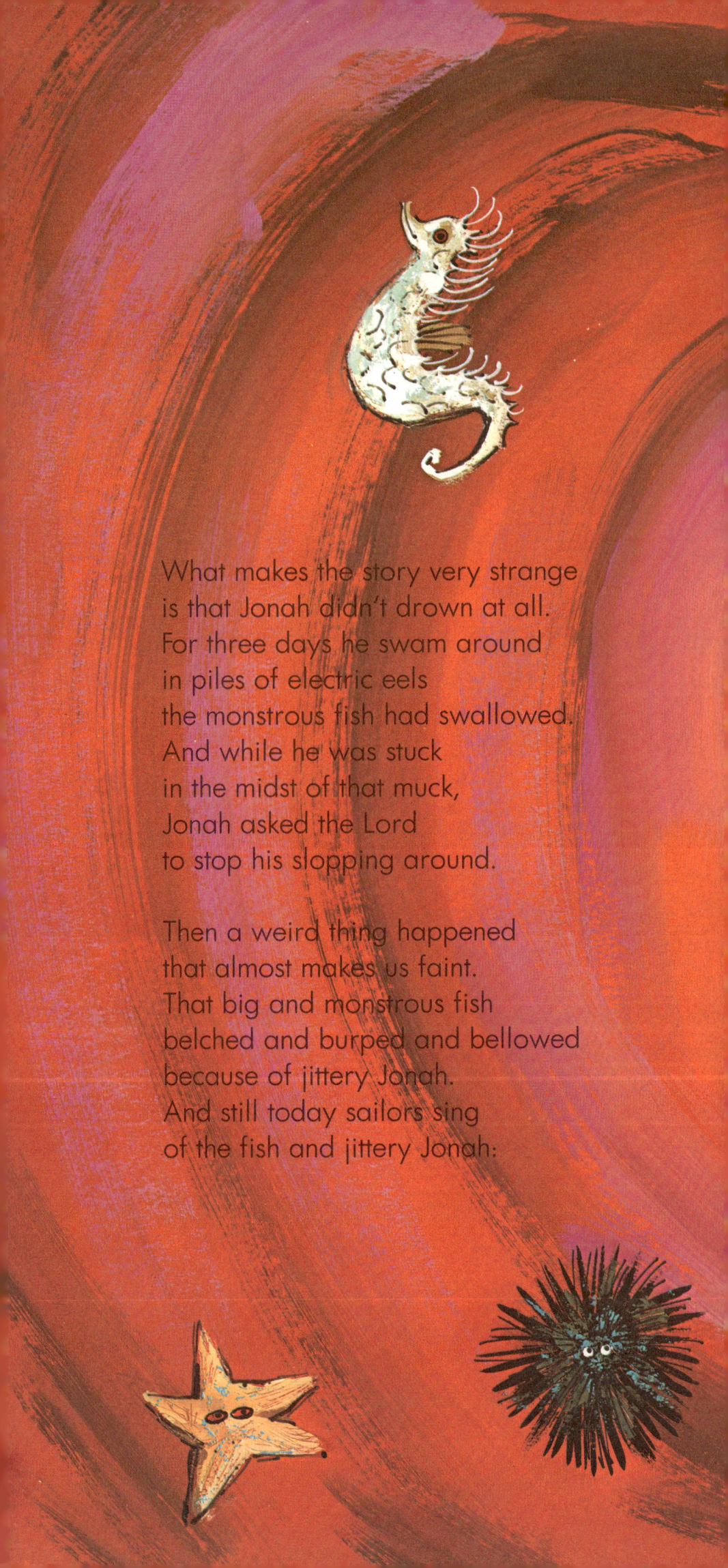

What makes the story very strange
is that Jonah didn't drown at all.
For three days he swam around
in piles of electric eels
the monstrous fish had swallowed.
And while he was stuck
in the midst of that muck,
Jonah asked the Lord
to stop his slopping around.

Then a weird thing happened
that almost makes us faint.
That big and monstrous fish
belched and burped and bellowed
because of jittery Jonah.
And still today sailors sing
of the fish and jittery Jonah:

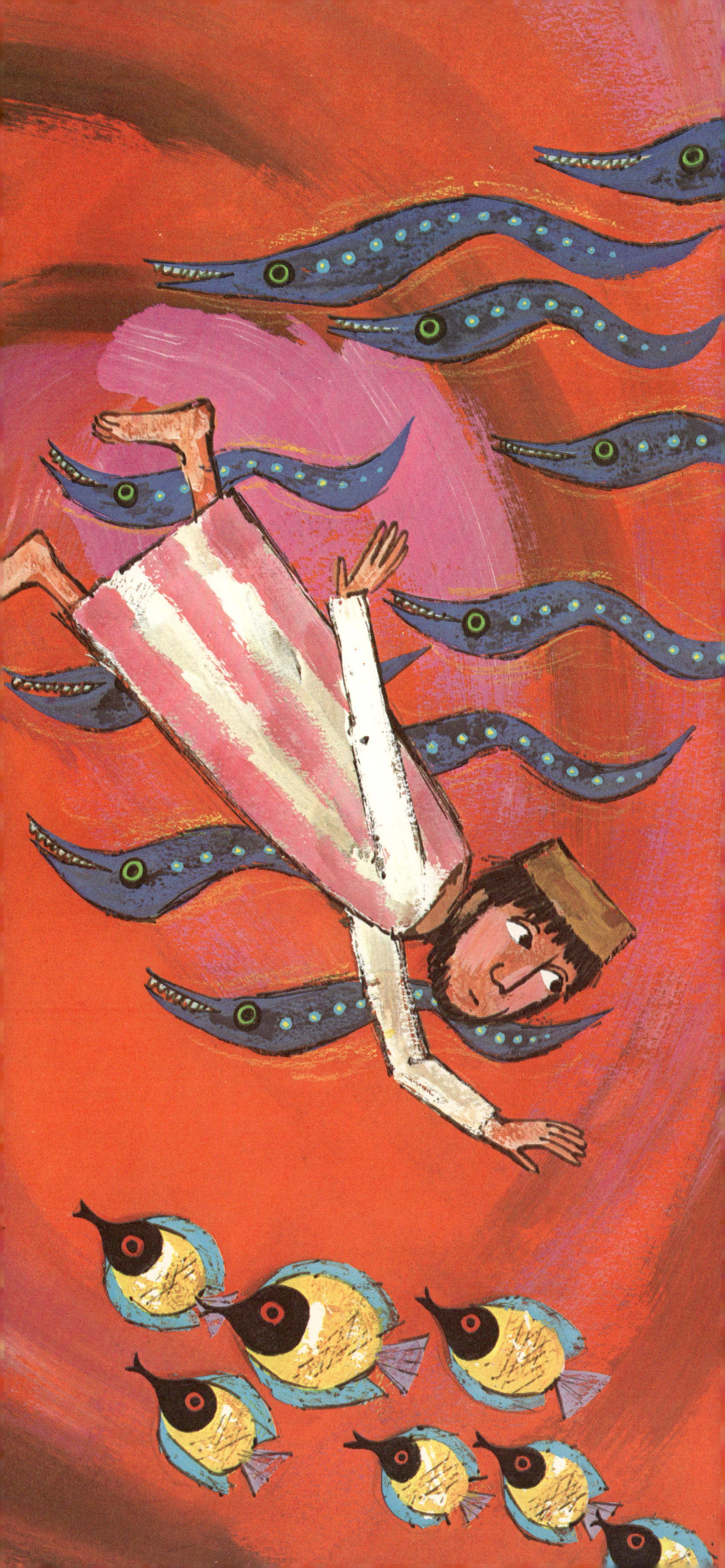

Monstrous fish with pains in his stomach,
Like a whale with pains in his stomach,
Roared and stormed with pains in his stomach,
Pains from jittery Jonah.
Ooops there, up comes Jonah.
Ooops there, out comes Jonah.
Ooops there, look at Jonah.
Messy, jittery Jonah.

The fish threw poor old Jonah up,
high upon the shore.
Jonah sat upon the sand
and smelled like rotten fish.

Then God said to Jonah, "Go!
Go and preach to Nineveh,
that great big, evil city.
And this time don't say No."
So Jonah went and preached
to that great big, evil city.
Jonah made it very plain
that God was coming very soon
to burn that city down.

Then a strange thing happened
that no one can explain.
Every man in that big city
and all the children, too,
changed their ways and turned to God,
to the Yahweh Jonah knew.

Jonah sat outside the town,
high upon a hill,
waiting for his God to come
and burn that city down.
He sat for hours in the hot, hot sun,
but Yahweh didn't come.

Then a weird thing happened,
right where Jonah sat.
A tall, green plant grew up,
as the beanstalk grew for Jack.
The plant gave Jonah shade
from the hot, hot, hot, hot sun.
And that made Jonah glad.

But a worm came up next day
and ate that plant
until it withered away.
And that made Jonah mad—
jumping, jittery mad.

And still today sailors sing
of the plant and jittery Jonah:

> Tall green plant from out of nowhere,
> Like a beanstalk out of nowhere,
> Cast some shade from out of nowhere
> Over jittery Jonah.
> One worm sucks at the beanstalk,
> One worm chews at the beanstalk,
> One worm kills off the beanstalk.
> Poor old jittery Jonah.

At last God said to Jonah:
"Why are you mad at Me
because I changed My mind
and didn't burn this city down?
Why are you sorry for that plant?
You didn't make it grow,
and now you want it back.

"Shouldn't I feel sorry
for all the people in this town
that I Myself have made?
Aren't they more important than a plant
that only lasts a day?

"Shouldn't I love them more
than you have loved your plant?
Well, Jonah,
what do you say?"

Will you sing this song?

    How many weird things have to happen?
    How many true words must be spoken?
    How many Jonahs have to suffer
    Before we learn God loves us?
    God's love reaches all men.
    God's love changes all men.
    God's love follows all men,
    Even men like Jonah.

OTHER TITLES

SET I.
WHEN GOD WAS ALL ALONE 56-1200
WHEN THE FIRST MAN CAME 56-1201
IN THE ENCHANTED GARDEN 56-1202
WHEN THE PURPLE WATERS CAME AGAIN 56-1203
IN THE LAND OF THE GREAT WHITE CASTLE 56-1204
WHEN LAUGHING BOY WAS BORN 56-1205
SET I LP RECORD 79-2200
SET I GIFT BOX (6 BOOKS, 1 RECORD) 56-1206

SET II.
HOW TRICKY JACOB WAS TRICKED 56-1207
WHEN JACOB BURIED HIS TREASURE 56-1208
WHEN GOD TOLD US HIS NAME 56-1209
IS THAT GOD AT THE DOOR? 56-1210
IN THE MIDDLE OF A WILD CHASE 56-1211
THIS OLD MAN CALLED MOSES 56-1212
SET II LP RECORD 79-2201
SET II GIFT BOX (6 BOOKS, 1 RECORD) 56-1213

SET III.
THE TROUBLE WITH TICKLE THE TIGER 56-1218
AT THE BATTLE OF JERICHO! HO! HO! 56-1219
GOD IS NOT A JACK-IN-A-BOX 56-1220
A LITTLE BOY WHO HAD A LITTLE FLING 56-1221
THE KING WHO WAS A CLOWN 56-1222
SING A SONG OF SOLOMON 56-1223
SET III LP RECORD 79-2202
SET III GIFT BOX (6 BOOKS, 1 RECORD) 56-1224

SET IV.
ELIJAH AND THE BULL-GOD BAAL 56-1225
LONELY ELIJAH AND THE LITTLE PEOPLE 56-1226
WHEN ISAIAH SAW THE SIZZLING SERAPHIM 56-1227
A VOYAGE TO THE BOTTOM OF THE SEA 56-1228
WHEN JEREMIAH LEARNED A SECRET 56-1229
THE CLUMSY ANGEL AND THE NEW KING 56-1230
SET IV LP RECORD 79-2203
SET IV GIFT BOX (6 BOOKS, 1 RECORD) 56-1231

the PURPLE PUZZLE TREE